Business Leadership: The Third Wave of Education Reform

Edited by Andrew Ashwell and Frank Caropreso

Conference Program Director
Leonard Lund

Ministry of Education, Ontario
Information Services & Resources Unit,
13th Floor, Mowat Block, Queen's Park,
Toronto   M7A 1L2

A Report from The Conference Board

The editors gratefully acknowledge the assistance of
Evelyn Samoré, whose editorial skills and unfaltering
professionalism were vital to the completion of this report.

Contents

FROM THE PRESIDENT v

WHO'S WHO AMONG CONTRIBUTORS vii

INTRODUCTION
Leonard Lund
The Conference Board xiii

PART I: BUSINESS LEADERSHIP

BUSINESS AND EDUCATION REFORM:
LOTS OF ACTION...ANY IMPACT?
Preston Townley
The Conference Board 3

A SENSE OF URGENCY, A HABIT OF PATIENCE
John L. Clendenin
BellSouth Corporation 7

PART II: INSTITUTIONALIZING BUSINESS INVOLVEMENT IN EDUCATION

EDUCATION SYSTEMS IN THE CORPORATION
Hedy White
International Business Machines Corporation 13

MANAGING EDUCATION RELATIONS
Carver C. Gayton
The Boeing Company 17

PART III: NEW STEPS TO IMPROVE THE BUSINESS/EDUCATION PARTNERSHIP

CHILDREN, SCHOOLS AND BUSINESS: A COMMON AGENDA
William S. Woodside
Sky Chefs, Inc. 23

COORDINATING HOUSTON'S CREATIVE CHAOS
Thomas H. Friedberg
Ranger Insurance Company 26

A NATIONAL EDUCATION POLICY?
Chester E. Finn, Jr.
Vanderbilt University 31

PART IV: CRITIQUING COMPACTS, COALITIONS AND COLLABORATIONS

THE BOSTON COMPACT REVISITED
James J. Darr
State Street Bank and Trust Company 37

THE CINCINNATI YOUTH COLLABORATIVE
Gordon C. Hullar
The Procter and Gamble Company 41

THE BALTIMORE COMMONWEALTH
Jon M. Files
Baltimore Gas and Electric Company 43

THE GREATER MILWAUKEE EDUCATION COMMITTEE
William L. Randall
First Bank Milwaukee 46

PART V: LINKING EDUCATION RELATIONS WITH HUMAN RESOURCES NEEDS

EDUCATION PROGRAMMING IN COMMUNITY
AFFAIRS DEPARTMENTS
Gayle Jasso
Security Pacific National Bank 53

EQUIFAX'S LEARN AND WORK PROGRAM
Charles F. Weiksner, Jr.
Equifax 55

THE HUMAN RESOURCES/COMMUNITY RELATIONS
TEAM APPROACH
Margaret M. McCann
Jocelyn Lewis
Brooklyn Union Gas Company 58

THE CORPORATE EDUCATION DEPARTMENT
Badi Foster
AEtna Casualty and Surety Company 61

From the President

The quality of our nation's education, linked directly to the quality of our workforce, has been pinpointed time and again as one of the keys to international competitiveness. Currently, the United States spends hundreds of billions of dollars on education. Yet, U.S. literacy ranks 48th out of 149 countries surveyed; and, unlike our competitors, we still don't have a national education agenda. Despite some isolated successes, many in business are concerned about our poor return on investment. Widespread education reform is far from being realized.

This concern was very much in evidence at the Board's 1989 conference on "Business Leadership: The Third Wave of Education Reform." Speakers and attendees shared insights gained from business/education partnerships that are being forged in cities across the nation. The talks in this volume reflect the highlights from that conference. I thank all the contributors for their pragmatic analyses and their enthusiasm in making the conference a resounding success.

Preston Townley
President

Who's Who Among Contributors

JOHN L. CLENDENIN, Chairman of the Board and Chief Executive Officer, BellSouth Corporation, Trustee, The Conference Board, Inc.

Mr. Clendenin began his telephone career with the Illinois Bell Telephone Company. He subsequently moved to the Pacific Northwest Bell Telephone Company in Seattle and to the American Telephone and Telegraph Company in New York. He was elected President of Southern Bell in April 1981. He became Chief Executive Officer of BellSouth in January, 1984, and named Chairman in April, 1984. He is a member of several corporate boards including RJR Nabisco, the Kroger Company, Coca-Cola Enterprises Inc. and First Wachovia. Mr. Clendenin is Vice Chairman of the U.S. Chamber of Commerce, Past Chairman of the National Alliance of Business, Chairman of the Education Committee of the Business Roundtable, and a member of the Board of Governors of the United Way of America. He has served as a board member of a number of other civic, educational and cultural organizations.

JAMES J. DARR, Vice President and Director of Community Affairs, State Street Bank and Trust Company

At State Street Bank, Mr. Darr is responsible for corporate involvement in the community, including grant contributions, public/private partnerships and media and government relations. He was previously Executive Director of Boston Private Industry Council from 1981 to 1987. Mr. Darr currently serves as Volunteer President of the Boston PIC.

JON M. FILES, Vice President—Management and Staff Services, Baltimore Gas and Electric Company

Mr. Files began his career with Baltimore Gas and Electric in 1957. From 1976 to 1978 he was Supervisor—Organization Planning, Corporate Staff Services; from 1978 to 1981 he was Manager—Corporate Staff Services. He assumed his current position in 1981. Mr. Files is associated with numerous professional and industrial organizations. He is a member of the American Compensation Association, the American Institute of Industrial Engineers and the American Society for Personnel Administration. Mr. Files is also Chairman of the Human Resources Management Division Strategic Planning Committee, Edison Electric Institute.

CHESTER E. FINN, JR., Professor of Education and Public Policy, Vanderbilt University; Director, Educational Excellence Network

Dr. Finn has recently reassumed his present position which he held from 1981 to 1985. From 1985 to 1988 he was Assistant Secretary, U.S. Department of Education where he headed the Office of Education Research and Improvement. Prior to 1981 Dr. Finn served as Senior Legislative Assistant to Senator Moynihan, Special Assistant to the Governor of Massachusetts and as staff assistant in the Nixon White

House, 1971 to 1972. He is the author of *Education and the Presidency, Scholars, Dollars and Bureaucrats* and numerous books and articles. In 1988 he was named chairman of the National Assessments Governing Board.

BADI G. FOSTER, President, AEtna Institute for Corporate Education, AEtna Casualty and Surety Company

Dr. Foster has been in his present position since 1981. He is responsible for corporate education programs ranging from human resource to data processing training. He also oversees Institute management consulting activities, educational technology and research, and AEtna's educational involvement with outside organizations. Dr. Foster came to AEtna from Harvard University. In his 10 years at Harvard, he held several positions including: Director of Field Experience Program, Graduate School of Education; and Assistant Director, J.F. Kennedy Institute of Politics. Prior to his tenure at Harvard, he held positions at Princeton, Rutgers, and the University of Massachusetts.

THOMAS H. FRIEDBERG, Chairman and President, Ranger Insurance Company

In addition to his position at Ranger Insurance Company, Mr. Friedberg is also President of Chase Reinsurance Management, Inc. and Executive Vice President of Chase Insurance Enterprises, Inc. Previously, he was President and Director of the two insurance companies and the general agency owned by United Van Lines, Inc. Prior to that he served as Senior Vice President of the Reliance Insurance Companies responsible for Life and Specialty Operations and as Senior Vice President, International Property and Casualty Operations for the Hartford Insurance Group. Mr. Friedberg began his insurance career in 1961 with CNA Insurance.

CARVER C. GAYTON, Corporate Director—Training and Education Relations, The Boeing Company

As Corporate Director of Training and Education, Mr. Gayton is responsible for establishing policy and coordinating employee development and training programs, as well as education relations programs and activities within the company. He was previously Administrator of Education from 1979 to 1981 at Boeing before he assumed his current position in 1981. Prior to that, Mr. Gayton was Director of Affirmative Action Programs at the University of Washington from 1969 to 1977 and Assistant Professor of Public Policy Administration, Florida State University from 1977 to 1979. Mr. Gayton is president elect of the Junior Engineering Technical Society, past chairman of Private Initiatives in Public Education and past Commissioner of the Northwest Association of Schools and Colleges. He is currently a member of the National Advisory Panel/National Center for Secondary Governance and Finance.

GORDON C. HULLAR, Reliability Manager, Product Supply, Packaged Soap and Detergent Division, The Procter and Gamble Company

Mr. Hullar has been in his current position since 1988. He is responsible for improving the reliability of the Product Supply System for his division. Previously, he held a number of assignments in engineering and manufacturing of soap, paper and industrial chemistry from 1960 to 1977. From 1977 to 1988 he subsequently held the position of Engineering Director, Toilet Goods; Plant Manager; Engineering Director, Bar, Soap and Household Cleaning; and Engineering Director, Packaged Soap and Detergent. Mr. Hullar is a member and chairman of the Private Industry Council and a member of the Cincinnati Youth Collaborative.

GAYLE JASSO, Vice President and Manager, Community Affairs Division, Security Pacific National Bank

Mrs. Jasso manages over a dozen California corporate volunteer and community education programs. These community involvement programs utilize thousands of Security Pacific employees and train over 4,000 high school and adult students per year. In 1986 Security Pacific's programs received President Reagan's Volunteer Action Award for Best Overall Corporate Effort. She received the award on behalf of Security Pacific from President Reagan at a White House ceremony. Her previous assignments with Security Pacific include Public Affairs Officer, (1976 to 1979) and Assistant Vice President, Community Educational Development Section (1979 to 1983). Prior to joining Security Pacific in 1976, she practiced public relations for a financial services company and taught high school English.

JOCELYN E. LEWIS, Educational Representative, Brooklyn Union Gas Company

Mrs. Lewis has been with Brooklyn Union since 1970 and in her current position since 1983. She is responsible for planning and coordinating Brooklyn Union's "Join-a-School" program activities with a local area high school as well as coordinating the educational services for schools within Brooklyn Union's service territory. Previously at Brooklyn Union she was Speaker's Bureau Coordinator where she managed the company's speakers' bureau and its film program. Mrs. Lewis is a member of the National Association of Corporate Speaker Activities and chairperson for the Erasmus Hall Community Advisory Council.

LEONARD LUND, Senior Research Associate, Corporate Relations, The Conference Board.

For the past twenty years, Dr. Lund has been concerned with issues such as local economic development, business-government relations, education, and public/private partnerships. He has been project director of seven Federally funded studies in such areas as environmental affairs, community economic development, corporate involvement with local governments, corporate location factors and in business/education relations. His latest study is Beyond Business/Education Partnerships: The Business Experience. Prior to joining the Board, he served for fourteen years as a senior researcher and business-government relations specialist for the New York Chamber of Commerce. Dr. Lund received a PH.D. in Public Administration from New York University in 1962. He has taught courses in municipal government and business government relations, corporate social responsibility and corporate urban economic development.

MARGARET M. MCCANN, Director of Employment and Recruitment, Brooklyn Union Gas Company

Miss McCann is responsible for hiring, college recruitment EEO/AA, the Medical Bureau and the Employee Assistance Program at Brooklyn Union Gas. Previous positions held there included Administrator, Management Recruitment from 1978 to 1980; Coordinator, Employee Benefits from 1980 to 1982; and Coordinator, Management Development in 1982. Prior to that she was an elementary school teacher for New York City. She assumed her current position in 1987. Miss McCann is a member of the American Gas Association, EMPL/EEO Committee, ASTD and ASPA.

WILLIAM L. RANDALL, Executive Vice President—First Bank Milwaukee

Mr. Randall is a member of numerous civic and community organizations. He is currently chairman of Greater Milwaukee Gives, member of the Trustee's committee of the Milwaukee Foundation and chairman of the Greater Milwaukee Committee Education Committee. He is a former member of the Governor's Commission on the Quality of Education in the Milwaukee Public Schools and a recipient of the 1987 Pro Urbe Award from Mount Mary College and the Governor's Award for Support of the Arts in Wisconsin.

PRESTON TOWNLEY, President and Chief Executive Officer, The Conference Board

Mr. Townley came to The Conference Board in 1988 after serving as Dean of the Carlson School of Management at the University of Minnesota, where he implemented a successful $40 million fund-raising effort and secured the second largest gift ever received by a U.S. business school. Prior to this, Mr. Townley was Vice President-General Manager of General Mills' largest division, Big "G", in 1973. In 1976 he became Group Vice President for Consumer Foods and in 1981, Executive Vice President, Consumer Foods. From 1976-1983, he managed Europe Foods (a seven-company complex). His tenure at General Mills also included responsibility for the Specialty Foods Group, New Business Development, the Golden Valley Division and the Marketing Services Group. Currently, Mr. Townley holds corporate directorships in Donaldson Co., TCF Financial Corporation, and QVS Properties, Inc. In 1967 Mr. Townley was selected a White House Fellow (one of sixteen chosen from a field of 1,200 applicants). He is currently the president of the Harvard Alumni Association.

HEDY WHITE, Director of Instructional Systems, International Business Machines Corporation

Ms. White joined IBM as a sales representative in 1973. She was promoted to sales school instructor in 1976 and then manager in marketing training in 1977. She advanced to delivery systems manager in the National Accounts Division, entry marketing education, in 1982. In 1984 she was named manager, instructional systems, IBM National Education. In 1986, Ms. White became Program Director, Curriculum Development, IBM Corporate Management and Employee Development. In 1987 she was named to her current position in IBM Corporate Education with the responsibility of expanding the use of instructional design and instructional technology.

CHARLES F. WEIKSNER, Jr., Vice President—Corporate Human Resources, Equifax, Inc.

Mr. Weiksner has been with Equifax since 1953 in both field and staff assignments and in his present assignment since 1981. The Corporate Human Resources Department at Equifax is responsible for four major areas: direct and indirect compensation programs, equal opportunity and recruitment in the Atlanta area, employee relations and generic training and development. A dotted line relationship exists with the operating companies human resources departments. Mr. Weiksner provides corporate direction, leadership, policies, processes, systems, and resources across the organization. He is a member of the Society of Certified Credit Association, The World Future Society and the Issues Management Association.

WILLIAM S. WOODSIDE, Former Chairman and Chief Executive Officer, Primerica Corporation, Chairman, Sky Chefs, Inc.

Mr. Woodside is currently a Director of Primerica Corporation, James River Corporation, Onex Packaging Company, and registered investment companies comprising 20 mutual funds of American Capital Family of Funds. He is President of the Board of Trustees of the Whitney Museum of American Art; former President of the Primerica Foundation; Chairman of the Institute for Educational Leadership, Inc.; Chairman of the Regional Plan Association of the New York-New Jersey-Connecticut Metropolitan Region; Co-Chairman of the School and Business Alliance of New York City; Vice Chairman Board of Trustees, Committee for Economic Development; a Director of Manpower Demonstration Research Corporation; and a Director of The Academy of Political Science. Mr. Woodside is also a Trustee of Barnard College; a member of the Board of Overseers, Harvard College, School of Public Health; a member of the Education Advisory Council, Carnegie Corporation of New York; Vice Chairman of the National Forum on the Future of Children and Their Families; and a member of the Business Higher Education Forum, and a Partner of the New York City Partnership.

Introduction

Education partnerships have grown from 42,000 to over 140,000 in the five-year period from 1983 to 1988. Almost 60 percent are business partnerships with local schools; primarily one-to-one, adopt-a-school programs with business providing speakers for school assemblies, underwriting awards to students and teachers, and contributing small amounts of financial assistance for various school needs. Interviews with business leaders in the preparation of The Conference Board report, *Beyond Business/Education Partnerships: The Business Experience*, disclosed general dissatisfaction with the results of these relationships, in such terms as "episodic," "fractionated," or "a short fix." The Board's research indicated that success in education reform resulted where business leadership could influence the policies of community-wide education coalitions, compacts and collaborations.

The 1989 conference examined two aspects of business leadership in education: how institutionalizing education policy and organization in the corporation affects corporate involvement in education reform; and how business leadership in selected cities has shaped the outcomes of education coalitions.

Speakers presented views of coalitions under development in New York and Houston, and progress reports on the Boston Compact, the Cincinnati Youth Collaborative, the Baltimore Commonwealth and the Milwaukee Education Committee. Leading corporate education executives also provided insights into the relationship between their company's education and training policies and their external school reform efforts, particularly the linkages between human resources and community relations—the two corporate functions usually responsible for maintaining education relationships.

In their views and comments on education reform, the conference participants strongly reflected the counsel of the keynoter, John Clendenin, who remarked, "It's more than handing out money. It's more than business being a partner in any effort. It's coming up with programs that can meet the needs of a city's youngsters, and pitching in to see that they work."

Significantly, as I moved among the 350 conference attendees, I heard discussions concerning the need to emphasize that education involvement should be considered a necessary investment for business; of school "choice" and school-based management programs as exciting new prospects for achieving education reform; of education reform as a national problem, high on the national agenda, for which national standards are needed.

                                                                Leonard Lund
                                                               The Conference Board

Part I

Business Leadership

Business and Education Reform: Lots of Action... Any Impact?

Preston Townley
President and CEO
The Conference Board, Inc.

Education is a top issue for business, not only because it relates to the quality and productivity of the workforce and the competitiveness of American industry, but because it is the single most important factor in fighting poverty, homelessness, drug addiction and crime. I am delighted that President Bush wants to make his the "Education Presidency." Let's hope so. But it is well to remember that only eight years ago another new President was advocating elimination of the Department of Education.

Today, business and government are continuing to commit enormous amounts of money, time and talent to education, including reform. All told, the nation now spends more than $185 billion a year on public education. Despite some promising pockets of success, however, there is growing concern that little true education reform has taken place. Most business/education partnerships, while well-intentioned, are localized, isolated and fragmented.

Education has been singled out as one of the keys to international competitiveness, but it is discomforting to note that in terms of literacy the United States ranks 48th out of 149 countries in a United Nations survey. And, unlike its competitors, the United States still has no national education agenda. U.S. business is worried because it faces the prospect of hiring a million new workers a year who can't read, write or count. BellSouth Chairman John Clendenin, a long-time champion of education change, has put it this way: "Workers qualified to fill the 20 million new information-age jobs this country will create before the century turns are becoming so scarce it's scary."

The scary part is the speed at which the job market is radically changing. Jobs once requiring only modest skills are evolving or disappearing. This trend will accelerate. A shortage of both educated and educable workers is having a major economic impact across the country. In New England, manufacturing growth is being stifled—not by demand, but by the lack of skilled workers or workers with the ability to learn the necessary new skills. The same pattern is developing in New York and other areas. It is a bitter irony that at a time of unprecedented high-tech affluence, virtually full employment and our highest level of mean education achievement, our school systems are producing so many "products" subject to recall.

To many business leaders, it has become almost impossible to overstate the urgency of education reform. Their interest is driven not by altruism but by enlightened self-interest. As David Kearns of Xerox declares: "Education is a bigger factor in productivity growth than increased capital, economies of scale, or better allocation of resources."

The bad news is the slow movement toward education reform. The good news is that a Third Wave of education reform is beginning to gain speed, offering the promise, if not yet the reality, of meaningful change. In this movement, vanguard companies are institutionalizing their education programs. Strong business leadership is insisting that education reform become a permanent element in corporate and school system goals. Some programs, such as the Boston Compact, are being re-evaluated and demanding something more: that in return for generous aid and the promise of jobs, schools get their test scores up and their dropout rates down. While the Boston Compact concept has generated controversy, it is serving as a model for many other cities. Business is making accountability an even stronger feature in the second stage of the Compact program. It is requiring schools to set stricter standards and goals that will be individualized for each grade and school.

Accountability is also the vital ingredient in a novel dropout prevention program in Minneapolis, sponsored by the Dayton-Hudson Corporation. The program provides incentives totaling $150,000 a year to a local high school when predetermined academic goals are reached. It is aimed at ninth graders most likely to drop out. The program, now in its third year, achieved its goals in the first two years. The full incentive payment was used to reward students, teachers, counselors, community workers and others who contribute to the program's success.

Increasingly, companies have concluded that for educational reform to succeed, schools must be restructured from the bottom up. That's why a rising number of companies are targeting more of their resources into elementary and secondary education. The list includes AT&T, American Express, IBM, General Motors, General Electric, Metropolitan Life and many others.

If some of today's trendlines seem alarming, it should be remembered that the First Wave of education reform was born of alarm. It was sparked by the 1983 report, *A Nation at Risk*, which painted a grim picture of America's future if the educational system did not improve. It led to a flurry of action. Companies by the thousands hurried to adopt schools. New partnerships were quickly created between business and education. The Second Wave featured a wide variety of company-sponsored programs, most of them designed to generate high visibility for individual corporations. While many companies were pleased with themselves, some began to ask tough questions, such as: Why is progress so slow? Are we really making a difference? How can we reach more schools and more students? Adopting schools and buying uniforms for school bands and basketball teams made some local people happy; but business leaders began to realize that this had little to do with true educational reform.

Steve Nielsen of Pacific Northwest Bell puts the partnership dilemma this way: "The crime that we have committed as a group of business people, generally speaking, is that we get involved in the cursory, low-level activities, partnering things that are nice, fun, easy and cheap. It isn't the answer: it's comfortable."

In today's Third Wave, aggressive efforts by business to promote improvements in local schools reflect a deep dissatisfaction with many existing partnerships. But business gained some invaluable experience during the first two stages of its involvement in education. Among the vital lessons learned are that business/education partnerships should:

• be permanently linked to long-term corporate policy and strategy.

• be viewed as pragmatic employment and training issues, not acts of charity.

• actively involve human resources executives in school curricula, identifying subject areas that have a direct impact on current and future jobs.

Fortunately, a growing number of major American companies now have thoughtful action plans. Most importantly, they realize that they are running in a grueling long-distance race, not a sprint. The real issue now is how to sustain interest and involvement over the long term in a nation that often views policy issues as trendy fashions—in today, out tomorrow. Ironically, these dilemmas may ensure business' success in generating systematic change.

Analyses and reports have been long on "What should be done?" and much less meaty on "How to do it." But there are encouraging signs—by shifting its focus from the strictly local level to the sources of political power, business leadership is mobilizing to stimulate real reform in our public schools. For instance, in my home state of Minnesota, the Minnesota Business Partnership financed a study of K-12 education in the mid-1980s and worked to get implementation of its recommendations through the legislature and governor. Today the state is viewed as a leader in innovative approaches, offering the first open school transfer policy.

Nationally, business is attacking the problem with great energy but action is still clearly localized and highly fragmented. Do we need a Sputnik-type jolt to move on a national basis? Are we too afraid of big brother, regulations, bureaucracy? Are we avoiding putting real clout against the problem?

In the long run, real success depends on all of us. Lasting reform will result from challenging those programs that are not working, and nurturing and supporting those that are. And applying real clout. The education issue clearly transcends old-time politics and frozen ideologies. True education reform wears neither a conservative nor liberal label.

While money has clearly proven to be no miracle drug, it will still be needed. With the overhanging problem of our national budget deficit, the response from the Federal Government is likely to be restricted, despite early enthusiasm in The White House. Business leadership may well have to step up its investment. But as Harvard's Derek Bok puts it: "If you think education is expensive, try ignorance."

A Sense of Urgency, A Habit of Patience

John L. Clendenin
Chairman of the Board and Chief Executive Officer
BellSouth Corporation
Trustee, The Conference Board, Inc.

While encouraged by improvements over the past five years, we are still disturbed by the state of education in this country and what that means for the future. Business faces a paradox of imperatives: urgency and patience. We need a sense of urgency because the problems in education threaten our economic and social health; we need patience because these problems are numerous and deeply rooted in the larger troubles of this society.

Business must be more actively involved on all fronts. It must be more involved in solving specific problems and in working more directly with educators, community leaders, and with youngsters as well as adults. At the same time, business must be a more forceful advocate for true reform. Our problems are so serious we cannot solve them with piecemeal efforts. We can alleviate them somewhat and make incremental improvements here and there; but we cannot adequately correct them without fundamental reform.

Today, we as a nation are more serious about the task of building an education system to fit the complexities of a world economy fed by information and communication. The evidence suggests that young people are taking more math and science courses, although they are still not taking or learning enough. Academic standards are generally more rigorous. Better students are going into teaching. States are increasing their education budgets. Interest is growing in providing greater assistance to disadvantaged children. Large and small businesses are seeking concrete measures they might take to become stakeholders in the schools in their states and communities. President Bush has pledged to be an education president. All this is good news, a reward for exercising patience.

On the other hand, I am a businessman deeply concerned when measuring the scale of improvements in education these past few years with the pace of change in technology and commerce. For those of us who deal with these changes daily, the pace is simply dizzying. But none of us would suggest that the scale of improvements in education has also been dizzying.

We want to provide our children and young people with schooling that will enable them to make the most of their potential; and we want to provide our nation with a workforce equal to the demands of a world economy. We must do all this not only for charitable reasons, but also because it is in our self-interest.

A sign of business' increased efforts on behalf of education is that many of us have institutionalized within the corporation a commitment to better schools. In the past, of course, we did this primarily through foundations that provide grants. More recently, we have begun to contribute in other significant ways. A recent conference in Chicago sponsored by Allstate looked at how various businesses are becoming genuine stakeholders in education. This is a healthy approach because business has far more to offer than financial support alone.

For example, some of the very best schooling in the United States today is provided by business. Note that I said "best schooling" and not "best education." There is a big difference between the two. The purpose of education far exceeds the scope of our schooling, which normally has a very tight focus. But much of our schooling is first rate, and wherever possible, we should turn it to good use in the larger arena of education.

At BellSouth, for example, we wondered what we might do to assist principals and other school administrators to become better managers. Study after study tells us that these leaders can be the critical element in a school's success or failure. Yet few school systems provide them with any systematic training. Management is seldom a strength in schools.

We decided to offer principals leadership training similar to that our rising managers receive. The response was tremendous. When you see the new enthusiasm of the principals who have undergone the course, you must believe that this program is already making a difference for children and young people in schools in BellSouth's nine-state region. Some principals have carried the ideas back to their own districts and passed them on to other principals and teachers. The program has become very popular. In fact, it is so popular BellSouth cannot keep up with the demand.

Some of the most impressive efforts beyond corporate financial contributions were spawned in New York. For example, The Academy of Finance offers high school juniors and seniors a two-year program that combines classroom instruction with on-the-job experience. Some 50 companies, including Oppenheimer, Salomon Brothers and Standard & Poor's, offer participating high schools everything from financial support to curriculum planning.

The academy was started in 1982 by American Express and Shearson Lehman Hutton working with the New York City schools. Ninety percent of its graduates have gone on to college—a result that was not necessarily intended. The program was aimed more at preparing these youngsters for a job right out of high school. A 90 percent rate of going on to college is the kind of unintended consequence we can all live with.

American Express now sponsors academy programs in 14 cities and is planning to establish a National Academy Foundation. Other businesses plan to join the effort and create other programs in addition to finance. This is precisely the kind of effort that moves beyond corporate giving.

Another impressive program is the Cincinnati Youth Collaborative, which is a community-wide effort that brings together educators, the private sector, and city government. The goal is to see that more of Cincinnati's young people learn the skills needed to make a better life for themselves. Businesses advise in curriculum changes and provide tutors, summer jobs, bridges to jobs, and last-resort financing for college education.

In Louisville, the business community was a moving force in creating an academy to train teachers and principals. The academy has become a hub for reforming and restructuring the local schools—a local think tank of sorts. A foundation to assist public education has been formed. Earlier, Louisville businesses raised money to make the Louisville-Jefferson County system one of the most computerized in America, and out of that effort other partnerships developed.

It takes patience in the face of failures and continually growing problems. We are seeing these partnerships of patience and persistence in Houston, Baltimore and Boston (whose Compact is emulated around the country). We are also dealing with basic literacy problems. We are doing more to persuade youngsters to stay in school by providing them with useful summer work and the incentive of a decent-paying job once they graduate. Such efforts involve more than handing out money and being a partner in any effort. They involve coming up with programs that can meet the needs of a city's youngsters, pitching in to implement these programs, and seeing that they work.

All these efforts are encouraging. They demonstrate what I meant in suggesting that our patience and our long-haul commitment dictate that we pursue specific remedies to specific problems. But urgent times demand reform, not just incremental change. These reforms, by the very dynamic they set in motion, should begin to correct the individual components of the larger problem.

What might such a reform be? One would be allowing market forces to work in our school systems. The means most discussed for applying the market mechanism in education would be to allow parents and children far greater flexibility in choosing a school. We generally call this "choice." There is criticism of the idea in some quarters. I join the critics in recognizing that it entails certain risks we would be obligated to guard against. But the approach is of the order of far-reaching ideas we must be willing to entertain. Our problems are so serious we cannot afford to exclude it automatically.

The idea can be manifested in many ways to fit local conditions and circumstances. For instance, perhaps some districts would allow more flexibility only within a school. Other districts or states might allow greater latitude. Minnesota allows parents to choose any public school in the state. We have not had time to assess how the idea is working. Similar programs are being considered in Arkansas and Massachusetts. East Harlem used its own variation of the idea for 15 years. School officials report that the percentage of students reading at grade level has risen from 15 percent when the program was started to 64 percent today. Other measures—graduation rates, percentage of students going on to college, test scores, etc.—are ambiguous. On the whole, however, the evidence suggests the idea has promise.

There are risks, but business-as-usual is also a risk—the risk of millions of youngsters with little chance of succeeding in this economy unless fundamental change occurs. Without economic opportunity there can scarcely be justice in the sense of a just society. Young people who do not have the skills to work at the good jobs created by today's technology will find few opportunities available—too little justice in their lives. The plight of these youngsters and the demands of a world economy should force us to continue looking for reform that would transform education from pre-school through high school. Our collective fate is bound up with their individual fates, and it is in our interest for them to succeed. Under the current system, many of them will not.

Part II

Institutionalizing Business Involvement in Education

Education Systems in the Corporation

Hedy White
Director of Instructional Systems
International Business Machines Corporation

In 1983, when *A Nation at Risk* caused quite a stir, IBM executives realized that business needed to assume more of a role in the training and educating of future workers. They expressed two major concerns: quality and the cost of education. Internally, IBM had to raise quality yet contain costs to better compete not only in the United States, but also with companies from abroad. The resulting restructuring of IBM's internal education was a revolution. The process that IBM underwent could potentially be used as a model to revolutionize school systems in the United States.

The first step in IBM's revolution was to establish quality measurements. It is very difficult in business to get a budget and resources, to hire and train personnel, if you cannot assure executives that they are getting their money's worth. Measurements are needed to chart progress, growth, and allay concern.

The second step was to establish standards for delivery systems. For a technology company not to use its own technology for training is ludicrous; yet we had no consistent standards for the use of our equipment in delivering education. In 1984, we established a corporate staff to oversee the task of revamping IBM internal education.

The corporate staff conducted an audit to establish a benchmark and found that IBM provided more than 12,000 courses internally. Seven thousand employees were assigned to teach IBM employees throughout the world. On any given day, 20,000 employees could be sitting in a class and, therefore, not on their job. That becomes important when you attach a cost per student, per day. Yet we could not measure the quality of education those 20,000 people were receiving.

We also found that the IBM educators had relatively low morale. There was no career path within IBM that encouraged talented employees to seek education as a career. If you want a truly dynamic, good education system, you must attract dynamic people.

From a cost standpoint, the first estimate from the audit was $600 million annually. After three months of research, we realized that the cost was really closer to $900 million. When student salaries are added—the time they spend in a classroom or at study as opposed to being on the job—the cost rises to $2 billion—about 4 percent of IBM's revenue. The question then arose: Is all that training necessary? The bottom line was a $200-million cut in the education budget. It became very clear that if we did not find a way to show a return on investment, we would be facing further cuts. That gets attention at IBM.

First, we looked at what we should do from a restructuring standpoint. We decided to move from an attendance-based to a performance-based evaluation system. Our reasoning: We educate to ensure growth. As IBM grows, processes must change to keep pace. Manufacturing processes are an example. Over the next few years, IBM will spend several million dollars preparing its manufacturing people in a program we call "The Production Employee of the Future." We will be teaching basic algebra, chemistry, physics, and some IBM-specific processes to about 22,000 plant employees. This is the kind of preparation required for us to ensure our growth over the next ten years.

We must also retain our flexibility. In a fast-moving industry like technology, IBM must be able to respond to the market. Education is an important part of that process. Our sales representatives, for example, must understand new ways of solving customer problems. Our engineers must be able to fix the products; our programmers must be able to develop the software. IBM has a full-employment policy. To maintain it, we must constantly retrain people to do new and different jobs. This not only gives us flexibility, but also allows us to maximize the human resources we have at IBM.

We knew we wanted to improve quality and to contain cost, and we knew we were going to do that not by monitoring attendance but by counting the skills acquired during training. This shift in focus was slow. At first, it was resisted by everyone except the top executives; they knew we had to get control of this process.

We chose a six-phase process. The first phase was to determine what education courses were needed. To accomplish this we identified specific jobs. We then created courses and curricula to provide the necessary skills those jobs required. We concluded that there were about 80 to 85 types of jobs at IBM—covering 90 to 95 percent of all jobs. Included are such jobs as secretary, programmer, marketing representative, systems engineer and first-line manager. Each of these jobs now has a curriculum in place. A manager determines what skills are needed to do the job, and assesses the employee's skills against these requirements. Eventually, every employee at IBM will be assigned an individual education plan that takes into consideration what each job demands and what each employee needs to learn to meet those demands. This approach has generated resources, as well as support from the executives, the staff and line management.

The second phase involved moving to a more structured education system. We have accomplished this in several ways. We use universities and outside consulting firms to advise us in implementing instructional systems development and design processes.

Third, we used our own technology. There will always be classrooms at IBM because we will always have the need for instructors to work one-on-one with students. We were able to use our technology to maximize that very critical resource of the instructor in the classroom. The centralized classroom costs us about $350 per student day. If all six million of those student days cost $350 a day, that would be unacceptable. By using a satellite system one expert can teach 150 to 250 people in remote locations. Therefore, a few IBM experts can transfer skills and knowledge in a more efficient way, costing us $175 per student day. This is an example of how technology is being used to leverage the expertise of our people.

Individual learning is also an important factor. Using the personal computers and the Infowindow system, we are able to teach what could not be taught even in the classroom. Still, technology does not replace the instructor. We use technology to bring the students' skill level up before the student meets with the instructor. Classroom and instructor time is used to achieve higher level skills, not just to deliver basic ones.

The fourth phase, designing a measurement system, is difficult; after two years, we are halfway there. We are working toward four levels of measurement. The first level is student reaction. Level two: Did they learn? (By the end of 1988, 95 percent of our courses were at this level.) Level three: Can they apply it on the job? (By the end of 1989, we will have that system in place.) Level four: How do we assure that business objectives are attained? If you cannot develop a business case for offering a course, then the course should not be given.

Another part of the measurement system is to measure the performance of the executives in charge of the schools. Previous measurements were based mostly on class size, tuition amount, and student reaction—did they find the course useful or not? The new measurements rely on strategic thrust: Is there a curriculum for each job? Do the executives sponsor that content? Are the employees trained according to the four levels of measurement? Was Instructional Systems Development (ISD) used to make sure that the education is high quality?

Fifth, we had to develop our own people. To improve morale, IBM provided our educators with career paths and added compensation. Now, there are executive jobs at IBM with such titles as Director of Instructional Systems and Vice President of IBM Education.

Sixth, we have attempted to integrate the education system into the entire management system. No longer is education a side thought; it is part of the plans, strategies and budgets of each of the lines of businesses, which keeps them involved in the process.

That is our systems education approach. How does it relate to business partnerships in K-12? As a complete entity, this may not work in K-12 or in higher education, but certain parts of it can certainly work: the change from an attendance-based to a performance-based system; the use of measurements so that there is accountability both on the student's part and on the system's part for providing the highest-quality education; the use of technology to leverage the professional skills of the teacher; and the systematic approach to developing and designing curricula. Those are basic processes that can work in any company, despite a company's size or objectives, and can work in K-12.

Managing Education Relations

Carver C. Gayton
Corporate Director, Training and Education
Relations
The Boeing Company

Prior to 1983, Boeing's involvement in K-12 education was minimal; our focus was on colleges and universities. This changed with the advent of such reports as *A Nation at Risk* and the creation of the Washington Round Table, an organization comprising 31 CEOs of major businesses within Washington state. The Round Table began to look into issues that affected the state's business climate. Over a period of three years, its members concentrated almost exclusively on K-12 education, because they believed this focus was directly related to the economic well-being of the state.

T. A. Wilson, Boeing's chairman at that time, headed the Round Table's education committee. He assigned a team of Boeing executives to identify what the company could do to assist schools. First, were any of Boeing's policies actually hindering relations with school systems? Our contributions policy targeted institutions of higher education. That had to be changed to incorporate *all* educational institutions. We also realized that our policies regarding employee involvement in various kinds of organizations, professional groups, etc., did not specifically mention educational institutions; so we revised them to encourage employees to become more involved in their local schools.

To allow executives to become more involved, we established a budget on the corporate level so that they could work with the school districts on focused projects that took significant periods of time. For example, an executive from Boeing Computer Services, one of our divisions, has been working with statewide school districts on utilizing technology in education.

Also, we agreed that there must be top-level management support for these programs. Early in 1984, our chairman sent a memorandum to all our company presidents indicating that they, their managers, and employees should become involved in local educational programs. Top-level management involvement is also shown by our management advisory committee on K-12 education. In addition to establishing a budget for our involvement with the schools, this committee specifies the criteria for determining the programs we will support, such as at-risk programs, the use of technology in education, administrative and teacher support, etc.

Each of our major facilities has an education manager who spends at least 50 percent of his time working with the local school district. The education managers talk to the superintendents of schools about what Boeing can offer and confer with the local chambers of commerce regarding prospective relationships with the school districts. It is important for education managers to be aware that each community and school district has its own culture and to adjust to these difference.

In order to be effective, we had to overcome some common misconceptions. For example, until recent years, there was some suspicion on the part of the education community regarding business' motives when they offer assistance. We also encountered some difficulty working with smaller businesses. They felt unable to compete with a company as large as Boeing in terms of what they could offer. We emphasized that each business is unique and has something to contribute to the schools. Today, at least six collaborative business/education partnerships have been established in school districts throughout the Puget Sound area as a result of the initiatives of our education managers.

Boeing has many corporate-wide programs that help our education managers do their job. For example, we have produced twenty-five 14-minute video tapes that depict the 25 most significant jobs at Boeing—word processing, drafting, electrical engineering, accounting, etc. Every high school in Washington has a set of these tapes. We developed the tapes because we learned that there is one guidance counselor for every 400 students in Washington. We thought the tapes could relieve some of the burden on the counselors and give students some guidance and information on jobs. The response to the tapes has been so positive that we now also make them available to community colleges throughout Washington and to our own employees.

Another video tape we produced is called "Attitudes: Goal Setting for Achievement." This tape addresses Washington's dropout problem: a 25 percent dropout rate from grades nine through twelve. It features various leaders—local celebrities, sports figures, artists, etc.—describing the importance of schooling and setting goals in their lives.

Boeing also has a "Computer for Kids" program, in which we provide computers to fifth-grade classes. The students in these classes work with their teachers to draft proposals on how computers can be used in the classroom and in their homes. A citizens' committee—made up of state legislators, business representatives, and community activists—review the proposals. The goal is to influence what is taught. So far, we are very pleased with this program, which is available to education managers to use within their districts.

To encourage other businesses to become involved in schools throughout the Puget Sound area, Boeing has offered to contribute $108,000 a year for mini-grant programs for teachers, and is encouraging other companies to donate money. These grants range from $25 to $500 for teachers to use in their classrooms. Review teams comprising representatives from the teachers unions, school administrations, and community groups review the proposals to determine those that would have the most positive impact on the classroom.

Another program we have been working on is called Scholarships for Engineering Students' Education (SENSE). Working on a pilot basis with the Seattle school districts and the University of Washington, we have identified schools that have a predominantly minority population and have selected students who show an inclination toward math and science. Boeing sets aside money for these students from their sophomore through senior years. When the students are accepted into a university or college, the money is made available to them. We began the program seven years ago, and all the students who started then went to college. Twenty-four students from this program are in college right now; twenty-one are majoring in math or science-related programs. Because of the success of this program, we are not only increasing the number of high school students getting support but we are also providing scholarships as the students go on to college.

We believe such partnerships provide a good foundation for building better bonds between businesses and educational institutions. Such bonds and feelings of trust are necessary to move deeper into the new wave of education reform. The business and education communities must work together to improve our schools; all of us lose if we do not.

Part III

New Steps to Improve Business/ Education Partnerships

Children, Schools and Business: A Common Agenda

William S. Woodside
Former Chairman and Chief Executive Officer
Primerica Corporation;
Chairman, Sky Chefs, Inc.

For several years, businesses in New York City have been involved in a variety of collaborative efforts with public schools. Some of these programs include Join-a-School, curriculum development approaches that use loaned executives, and mentoring programs that match students with professionals. While each of these programs has made a contribution, problems still exist. Too many students are not receiving an education that prepares them for college or for entry-level jobs.

In 1986, Governor Cuomo and the State Legislature created the School and Business Alliance (SABA). Its mission: To promote business sector support of public schools by bringing together educators, business people, government representatives, labor leaders and advocates. Fourteen local SABAs were established throughout the state.

The New York City SABA program has three parts: New York Working, Learning and Mentoring. New York Working focuses on improving opportunities for the successful employment of students. New York Learning provides support for effective educational practices in the schools. New York Mentoring acts as a clearinghouse for the 200 mentoring programs already in place, trains mentors and is developing programs to encourage parental involvement.

New York Working

New York Working is a joint venture between SABA and the New York City Partnership. Operating in six high schools during its first year as a pilot project, New York Working provides career and employment services to students who plan to enter the labor force upon completion of high school.

The six high schools involved reflect the cultural, socio-economic and demographic diversity of New York City. The schools operate year-round career development and employment centers that recruit businesses to work with schools, develop better career education for students and help students find jobs. As a result, over 300 students were placed in jobs within the first two months of the program. Currently, a major effort is underway to integrate career education into the 9th-12th grade curriculum in a way that consistently exposes students to the business world. While we have a long way to go, the early results indicate that New York Working is on the right track.

New York Learning

New York Learning proposes to support school-based improvement by building a bridge between the latest education research and the real world of the classroom. Its emphasis is on teaching students the teamwork, communication and problem-solving skills that will be required of them in the workplace.

New York Learning recognizes the expertise of those who serve on the front line every day—the teachers. Its fundamental premise is that the regeneration of the school system can be built upon the foundation provided by model programs that are already in place. Perhaps the most eloquent testimony of this solid foundation is that 100 out of 300 semi-finalists in last year's annual Westinghouse Science Talent Search came from the New York City public school system.

In order to encourage teachers to develop methods that teach youngsters to work together, New York Learning will award small grants for experimentation and innovation in the classroom. A fellowship program will provide opportunities for service and personal growth to outstanding teachers and administrators in the school system.

New York Learning will disseminate what has been learned from its activities and other programs through publications, conferences and leadership seminars. It is imperative that teachers, principals and other administrators work together if they are to successfully apply new ideas. A critical factor in the development of this program has been the cooperative relationship involving the Board of Education, district superintendents, the United Federation of Teachers, and the Council of Supervisors and Administrators.

New York Mentoring

In New York City, representatives from more than 100 organizations—including corporations, professional organizations and colleges—serve as role models for students in the public schools. These mentoring programs connect students to adults who can teach them the social and job skills required to succeed. Almost all the programs operate on a shoestring and most are the brainchild of a single employee committed to helping youngsters.

New York Mentoring's mission is to provide technical assistance to mentoring programs, training and preparation for mentors, and other program support services. It will also create a computerized data base of all mentoring programs in New York City so that programs can more easily share information and recruit volunteers. Finally, it will conduct research on effective mentoring practices and strategies and will investigate some of the urgent issues facing the mentoring movement.

One of those issues is parental involvement. Parents need to become involved in the schools and be made a part of the educational development of their children. They need to know that they have much to contribute. Educators often complain that parents are not doing their share to help assure their children's success. Parents, on the other hand, often complain that they are barred from participating effectively in their child's education. Some mentors have been able to complement parental involvement in the schools. Teachers also need to become more involved in school decision making. Principals need to be given greater control over resources if they are to be held accountable for their school's performance. Many factors influence a school's success or failure, but the most important is the leadership qualities of the principal and the superintendent.

Finally, we must not forget that businesses and schools have very different organizational cultures. They function differently. Their people speak different languages. Business/education partnerships may, therefore, be difficult; but they are absolutely crucial. They are here to stay, but only if everybody works hard at making them succeed.

Coordinating Houston's Creative Chaos

Thomas H. Friedberg
Chairman and President
Ranger Insurance Company

The phrase "creative chaos in Houston" was coined a year ago and appears in a recent Conference Board report. We in Houston like to emphasize the "creative" rather than the "chaos." By not trying to define the one and only way to have a business/school partnership, we have allowed a great deal of creativity to be brought to this issue.

There are about 30 independent school districts in the Houston area. The Houston Independent School District (HISD) makes up about 40 percent of the student population. The students are 41 percent Black, 41 percent Hispanic, and 18 percent "other." In contrast, the faculty is 45 percent Black, 8 percent Hispanic, and 47 percent "other." Considering our geographic location, there is an ever-increasing number of Hispanic students in our school system and in our community in general. The student population totals about 190,000 and there are 233 campuses. The budget totals $700 million. More telling, perhaps, is the fact that 53 percent of all students are on a free or reduced lunch program, and 18 percent have limited English proficiency. At the elementary school level, the numbers are even more frightening: 73 percent are on a free or reduced lunch program and 23 percent have limited English proficiency.

The high school dropout rate is 17 percent, but we have high schools ranging from one that produces as many National Merit scholarships as any school in the country to others whose average SAT scores were in the low to mid 700s—a 700 means less than 30 percent right in both the math and verbal portions of the exam. On the Metropolitan Achievement Tests, given to grades 1-9 in the Spring of 1987, Houston scored at or close to the national median through the fourth grade. Thereafter, we begin to drop below the national median at an ever-increasing rate. The average expenditure per pupil in 1987-88 was $3,132.

With this background, it is no wonder many people have become more and more concerned about education in the Houston area. The Mayor's Hearing on Youth led to a project called Youth 2000. It focused on the fact that students entering grade school in 1988 would be high school graduates by the year 2000. The Greater Houston Chamber of Commerce adopted the education issue as its main theme and formed three working committees that have led to some exciting developments in the business/school partnership area. The number of partnerships in Houston grew from 17 in 1980-81 to 425 in 1986-87. Today there are 597 partnerships and 2000-plus business people involved. As always, some programs are more extensive than others, but every effort is worthwhile.

Perhaps the most significant activity in the partnership area was the development of the Houston Business Promise (see page 28). The K-12 issues committee of the chamber of commerce was a driving force behind this effort. It culminated in an announcement early in 1989 of the Business Promise at a press conference attended by the mayor, the superintendent of schools, representatives of the chamber of commerce, and the business community at large. The Promise is a commitment by business to help in seeing that every child in the Houston area receives a quality education.

The Business Promise is about more than partnerships, and so is the overall effort in Houston. Youth 2000 has directed its efforts at several specific areas. The project called Adopt provides low-cost, after-school care for elementary school children at 26 HISD campuses throughout Houston. Children in the program remain at the schools from the end of the school day until 6 P.M. Nonprofit organizations such as the YMCA and the YWCA, the Child Care Council of Greater Houston, the Gulf Coast Community Services Association, and Campfire actually operate the programs. HISD provides a certified teacher at each site to tutor and assist students with homework and enrichment activities. Fees for the after-school program are based on family income and do not exceed three dollars per day. About 1,000 children are currently served by the program. The goal is to increase the number of sites at a rate of five per year.

Communities in Schools is a private nonprofit organization that coordinates the efforts of over 13 social service agencies and public education personnel to reduce the dropout rate in HISD. In addition, 17 elementary schools participate in Project CHARLIE, a drug abuse prevention program. Communities in Schools provided pre-employment skills training and summer work for 400 youths in 1987. The goals are to expand at a rate of two sites per year and to make Project CHARLIE available at all 164 elementary schools.

Other programs deal with teenage pregnancy, dropout prevention, and the prenatal to six-years-of-age development period. These programs are in

The Houston Business Promise

We believe that every child in the Houston area should receive a quality education. Furthermore we believe that literate, thoughtful and effective citizens are critical to fulfillment of individual lives and of families, to a healthy competitive economy and to a viable democracy. We, as responsible adults, have both the privilege and the duty to prepare our young people to assume responsibility for the future of our community and nation by assuring a strong education system.

While the primary responsibility for educating our young people lies with our education system and within the family structure, the business community is uniquely positioned to reinforce these responsibilities through corporate policies and programs which will help assure that every child in the Houston area receives a quality education. Therefore:

hereby adopts this Houston Business Promise and will communicate to all of our employees our commitment to quality education. We will:

★ Encourage employees with children to support and be involved in the learning process of their children, including attendance at parent/teacher conferences.

★ Support a school or schools through a meaningful partnership effort including employee volunteer involvement; sharing of expertise, facilities and equipment and/or financial assistance. This may range from adopting a school to participating in existing programs.

★ Assist in preparing students for the workforce. This may include providing information in the classroom and exposure to the workplace through plant/office visits and summer or part-time jobs.

★ Assure graduates of Houston area high schools the opportunity to interview for available jobs. Increase student awareness of job opportunities and requirements through school career days and other appropriate means.

★ Support the recruitment and retention of high quality teachers and administrators. This may include summer jobs for teachers, small financial grants to assist teachers in classroom projects, teacher and/or administrator recognition, and other programs in support of this goal.

★ Encourage students to pursue education beyond the high school level.

★ Encourage employees without high school diplomas to complete the requirements for a diploma or the equivalent.

★ Endeavor to be informed and communicate with employees on important educational issues.

The Greater Houston Chamber of Commerce

_____   _____
Company Representative   Chairman, GHCC

Date: _____

various stages of development. "I Have A Dream" is also operating in one school in Houston. The Houston Business Committee for Educational Excellence uses a relatively small amount of contributed funds to reward outstanding teachers and most-improved students, to send principals to academies at Harvard and Texas A&M, and to award small grants to teachers and principals who submit innovative proposals. This year we will award about 125 teacher grants at $250 each.

Finally, another Houston activity is Executive Class Day. Many of us spent March 8 meeting with students, teachers, and principals to develop a better understanding of what is going on in the schools. Last year 64 senior executives of Houston businesses participated in Executive Class Day. You cannot begin to comprehend what the problem is until you get into a school yourself. We recently spent Saturday morning tutoring seventh graders in preparation for their mandated achievement tests. Two of my senior vice presidents and general counsel participated, and at a wrap-up session afterward, one of them said that it is difficult to teach how to find a least common denominator when students don't even know their times tables.

We are trying to bring some coordination to the process. All of the business/school partnerships are coordinated through a department in the school district. There is a director of business/school partnerships who handles all the assignments. So the image of all the businesses descending upon the schools randomly is not quite accurate, although no two approaches are the same. In addition, the K-12 issues committee of the council is putting together a matrix of all the activities going on, be they business/school partnerships or community-based efforts, to determine how well a particular area in the city is being serviced. Each high school is being fed by a couple of middle schools, which in turn are being fed by several elementary schools, and we are going to try to get a balanced approach in terms of these extra services. This will serve as a backdrop for the assignment of future partnerships.

As a result of the Business Promise, which has been signed by over 200 companies, the Committee on Business/School Partnerships will try to develop partners to meet specific needs. When a company signs the partnership, it is not just left up in the air. The company is called on by people who will delineate options, find out where the interest lies, and suggest appropriate outlets. While we cannot tell a company where to go or what to do, we do try to direct it to where the greatest need exists. This movement toward more involvement with the schools is obviously in sync with what is going on throughout the country.

Several questions are always asked: Is this activity wanted by the schools? The answer is yes, although not always to the same degree. You must have the right match-up of principals and teachers. We ran 60 students through some remedial math and English last summer at our building with teachers from the school with which we worked during the school year, and during one of the sessions, they did not want any volunteers. Some of the teachers are still very protective of their classrooms; they see them as their turf. This is something we in business have between departments every day.

Is it working? We see some improvement in test scores. Is it something we in business should be doing? I believe it is. We are not necessarily in the business to educate, but most of us are spending much more than we would like to educate our employees so they can be more effective for us.

A National Education Policy

Chester E. Finn, Jr.
Professor of Education and Public Policy
Vanderbilt University;
Director, Educational Excellence Network

There ought to be a national education policy. I am a relatively recent convert to the proposition that it is time we look across the whole country in relation to what our kids are coming out of school knowing and, in far too many cases, not knowing.

First, I want to distinguish national from federal. Congress should not become the nation's school board and the Secretary of Education should not become the nation's school superintendent. That is alien to our constitutional arrangements and unrealistic with respect to financing. U.S. spending on elementary and secondary school education is gaining on $200 billion a year, of which the federal government currently supplies 6 percent. The states supply 50 percent and the localities 44 percent. For the federal government to supply any significantly larger share than 6 percent—the all-time high was 9 percent—would require a fundamentally different economic and budgetary situation, which no one foresees for the near future.

The real story of the current wave of education reform is the leadership of the states. It involves the shift in control and authority for the big education decisions and for the bulk of the education dollar from the localities to the states. History is going to regard this as a seismic change in the basic governance arrangements of U.S. elementary and secondary education during the 1980s.

On the whole, it has been a good occurrence. But we continue to come in last, or nearly last, in every international comparison. According to the National Assessment of Educational Progress (the nation's report card), only 6 percent of high school graduates can read at college level. Only about one in five can write at a barely adequate level. Fewer than one in ten can handle multi-step math problems and problems involving algebra or a basic knowledge of scientific concepts. Two-thirds of the eleventh graders tested could not place the Civil War in the correct half century, although practically all of them were taking U.S. History that year.

This is the population that is succeeding in American education, making it through the schools, and going on to college. We have all kinds of data and testimonials from employers about the state of their employees, including those who graduate from high school. Much of the information from our colleges is pretty grim about the state of their entering freshmen and the prevalence of remedial and compensatory programs for people who make it into college. A large part of American higher education has become remedial secondary education in which students are being taught what they should have learned in high school.

We are spending more on elementary/secondary education than ever before—about $4,800 per student on average—but we do not get the same product for the money spent. The desired end product is not being spelled out by the system. Obviously, the product would not have to be specified for the whole country; some states are beginning to specify what they would like their students to know before they get out of secondary school. California, in my opinion, is leading the pack in this regard. New York State is doing a decent job, at least on paper. But in a large, mobile society like ours, the product ought not to be so very different from state to state.

Therefore, I favor the idea of a setting national goals or norms for the minimum acceptable level of skills and knowledge that everyone should have upon exiting a formal or compulsory education system. I would make attaining that minimum set of norms or goals the precondition for completing a formal or compulsory education. One of the most bizarre aspects of our society is to have high school graduation occur at age 18 but to allow 16 year olds to decide whether or not to stay in school. I do not think 16 year olds are the best qualified people in this society to make decisions about what is in their long-term best interest.

We must rethink the notion of compulsory education and have it not relate to age levels but to attainment levels. When you have learned what you need to learn, you can decide whether or not to stay in school and learn even more. So national goals or norms ought to be developed by a consensus-seeking process. Some advice to Mr. Bush: Catalyze that process with the help of the governors and concerned laity around the country. These norms should be voluntary for states and localities to adopt as they wish. I am well aware that this, nevertheless, portends a kind of national core curriculum, but I do not think that is so bad, as long as it is not the entire curriculum. One of William Bennett's (Former Secretary of Education in the Reagan administration) parting shots was a publication called *James Madison High School*, in which he set forth a recommended high school curriculum for the country. About 75 percent of the curriculum he suggested would be identical for everybody; the other 25 percent would be the domain in which kids could choose electives, schools choose specialties, and states and localities add their particular emphases and concerns. You could have a good debate about whether that uniform core ought to be 62 percent or 79 percent or how much of the total should be coming to everybody. I believe 75 percent is just about right.

In the 1983 report, *A Nation at Risk*, the commission suggested that every high school student take the "new basics:" four years of English; three years each of math, science, and social studies; two years of a foreign language; and half a year of computers. Only 13 percent of high school students graduating in 1987 actually took that program of courses. If you lop off foreign language and computers and just look at four years of English and three years each of math, science, and social studies, the graduating classes of 1987 consisted of 30 percent who achieved that program of study or better, and it was not equitably distributed. About 30 percent were white; about 22 percent Black and Hispanic; and 54 percent Asian. A partial explanation for the Asian success story is what they studied while in school.

National goals and norms can alter this situation, but these goals and norms should relate not just to basic reading and writing skills, but must include math, science, history, geography, civics, literature and foreign languages. We are capable of talking about these things at a minimum level of attainment, about what that minimum should be, and about the best way to determine how many people have achieved that level, and what ought to happen to those who do, and to those who do not. If we are clear about it with respect to secondary education, we must be clear about it in kindergarten. Otherwise, we will be in for many unhappy surprises, which would not be fair to the kids or to the educators.

We already have a sort of *de facto* national curriculum. It is pretty shoddy; we backed into it. It is compounded of the products of the textbook companies; the testing industry; the TV industry; the popular culture; music, movies, and magazines; the fast food companies; and the national publications. It is also compounded by the efforts of the professional education associations, of which there must be two trillion, and of their journals and meetings. It is time to turn this creeping sameness into a virtue by getting clear about the results we would like to achieve.

As for the federal government, most of what Washington itself continues to do is likely to be very similar to what it has done these past 20 years or so. Most of the money is likely to be spent on such programs as Chapter One and Headstart, on statistical research, on the enforcement of civil rights, on college student aid, etc. I think the fundamental role of Washington is not likely to change very much, which is probably as it should be. Again, this is the distinction between national—in the sense of nationwide—and federal, which will continue in much the same direction.

Some cautions about what I have been saying: First, I am not only talking about factual knowledge but also about people's ability to use information to think, analyze, and reason. I am not content with skills only; many educators are drifting into a mindset that as long as people acquire learning skills, it does not matter whether or not they actually know anything. The knowledge/skills tradeoff is the wrong tradeoff. Knowledge is to skills as bricks are to mortar: If you want a sturdy wall, you need both, and neither by itself will give you much of a wall.

Second, the purposeful national curriculum I have suggested would not be a static curriculum. It would represent our population, society, and culture. We have an assimilating, inclusive, and changing culture that will continue to change, and the curriculum should change with it.

Third, while testing, measurement, and assessment will be needed to know how we are doing, not everything we care about is amenable to traditional testing of the multiple choice, machine-readable variety. New assessment approaches will cost a little more than we are accustomed to spending.

Fourth, I have been talking about the academic core; for the record, I know that that is not all that schooling is about. Schools also involve a hidden curriculum of values, character, attitudes, and habits that are just as important. We cannot stop thinking about that hidden curriculum even as we get more purposeful about the cognitive core. Schools will and should differ from each other outside this core. The more they differ, the more important it is to allow people to choose among them on the basis of those differences. Schools should differ outside the core as to curriculum and across the entire curriculum with respect to the pedagogy, the organization, the style, the structure, and the configuration of the school.

Finally, an important distinction is that policy makers should be in charge of the results of education and educators should be in charge of the means of education—the steps by which those ends are achieved. We are indeed careening toward a *de facto* national education policy. We might as well make it a purposeful one, the one we want. Design the product and then get about the business of producing it.

Part IV

Critiquing Compacts, Coalitions and Collaborations

The Boston Compact Revisited

James J. Darr
Vice President and Director of Community Affairs
State Street Bank and Trust Company

Business involvement in the Boston school system began in 1975, when a federal district judge ordered the desegregation of the city's public schools. Encouraged by the judge and local political leadership, twenty or so companies linked up with individual high schools to show that they cared during this civic crisis. These "adopt-a-school" pairings were embraced—not because anyone had a real sense of what business ought to do—but because they were a sign of progress. They were good news for a system that really needed good news.

Over the next six years, however, this "good news" stage became a fairly disillusioning experience. By 1981, the school desegregation crisis was over, but the news about the schools was in some ways worse than ever. In the span of 14 months, there were four school superintendents. The school system budget was frozen for a couple of years, and about 20 percent of the teaching force was laid off. There were several embarrassing and well-publicized incidents, including the arrest, trial, and jailing of one of the five elected school board members. The image of the Boston public schools fell to an all-time low.

It was at this time that the second stage of business involvement in education began. In 1981, the Boston Private Industry Council—a business-led, nonprofit organization started a few years earlier—began a summer job program. It did so not because there was a desperate need for summer jobs in Boston—we already had a massive program that was employing 4,000 to 5,000 youths—but because business leaders realized that the only way to address youth unemployment in the long run was through improved education. It occurred to them that they should try to hire some youngsters, not just to give them jobs or wages, but to give them exposure to the corporate world.

This summer job program had three features that made it different from other school/business collaborations: First, it was not a one-to-one, company-to-school program, but rather involved an intermediary—in this case, the Private Industry Council (PIC). Second, it asked companies to submerge their individual identities and work together. Finally, it rewarded students not simply on the basis of need, but also on the basis of their performance and attendance records.

With the success of this program in 1981—and as the business community subsequently became more and more involved in the public schools—the notion of a citywide effort to improve the overall quality of education in Boston began to take shape. In the fall of 1982, the Boston Compact was unveiled. In essence, the Compact gave priority in hiring to public school graduates in return for measurable improvements in the school system. Improvement was to be measured in five ways: better test scores, better day-to-day attendance, a reduced dropout rate, higher proportion of graduates going on to full-time employment, and a higher proportion going on to college.

Many business leaders doubted they could find jobs on the scale demanded by the Compact (the unemployment rate in Boston at that time was 9.5 percent). Of course, they also wondered if the schools would live up to their side of the bargain.

Nevertheless, from 1982 to 1986 the Compact had a good run. Each year, there were developments and additions. In 1983, there was a University Compact that added another layer to the effort; in 1984, there was a Compact with trade unions, brokered by the new mayor who had good connections with organized labor; and, in 1985, one of the companies in New England began, through an endowment, a scholarship program for Boston school graduates. This scholarship program now has $6 million of endowment. The overall effort to raise private money for the schools now is about $15 million.

By 1986, however, it became clear that one of the five goals was not advancing: the dropout problem. A conference was organized to bring more attention to this issue. In the Summer of 1986 the school superintendent and the mayor signed an agreement to engage in a series of steps to reduce the dropout rate. One of those steps was to expand a program that had begun a couple of years before—a ninth grade, first-year-of-high-school intervention program—through the Private Industry Council.

By early 1987, the mood of the city had begun to change. The rising dropout rate emphasized how poorly, in some respects, the schools were doing. The system went through a whole string of crises: burning schools, bus strikes, etc. The elected school committee members were constantly fighting among themselves at their public meetings. A newspaper characterized one meeting in December of 1986 as a circus. The city council and the mayor began to talk about replacing them.

In 1987, in the midst of these troubles, Boston began to move into the third stage of business/school partnerships. The business community began to work behind the scenes to change some of the laws that governed education. Business leaders worked with the mayor and the school board to develop a home rule petition. Subsequently passed by the state legislature, the home rule petition changed the powers of the school committee and gave the superintendent more authority to hire and fire and to sign contracts. It changed the budget cycle and mandated certain dates by which things had to be done. It was a departure for the business community to be involved in the political struggle to change the school system.

Later in 1987, the business community, the mayor, the superintendent, and various other parties began a formal review of the Compact. The results were monitored and assessed; committees were established, and well into 1988 there were new goals that were put on paper. By June 1988, there was a package of new goals on which all the parties agreed. The notion of the new package was not just to renew or continue the Compact, but to recreate it.

The business community felt, however, that certain fundamental changes in the political system had to be made before these education goals could be reached. These changes involved the redistribution of power. How much power should each of the three levels have—the administration or the elected school board, the individual schools, and the parents? Business felt that there was a paralysis of power in Boston, that important decisions were not being made or were being delayed for months, and that the people who managed or administered the system were not willing to make the tough decisions that had to be made. Before the Compact could be renewed, these things would have to change.

Last Halloween, when the Chairman of the Boston PIC announced that the business community was not going to sign up for another five years of the Compact, it was seen by some as an example of business backing off from involvement in the city's schools. Actually, we in the business community felt that by saying no at that moment to the Compact, we could create leverage for change. We had entered into this new and important third stage that I call "real news." The business community is now involved in a true fight for the future of the Boston public schools.

But it is not business alone; it is business sharing certain views and goals with teachers, parents, politicians, and others in the community. We are trying to see some real change come about from the redistribution of power. For instance, this might involve giving parents a choice in the school their children attend. In Boston this is known as the Student Assignment Plan. Last week, under much pressure, the school board approved the plan. It remains to be seen whether the plan can be implemented, but at least it shows a decentralizing shift of power toward the parents and the individual schools.

Finally, there is a question about what power should remain at the city-wide policy-making level. Last fall, the mayor put together a blue-ribbon panel of 11 members. The panel, in which I participate, may recommend abolishing the elected school board—as happened in Chicago—and replacing it with an appointed school board. The primary goal is to make the mayor accountable for the quality of education and not dilute that accountability through a separate elected structure. If the schools are the most important city service, the chief elected official should be the person responsible for the quality of the schools.

The deadline for signing the Compact—and for seeing progress on school-based management, parental choice, and city-wide decision making—is at the end of March. It could be that if progress has not been made, the Compact itself might disappear with the underlying programs continuing on. That might not be a bad thing, because I think we are now in a more mature stage of the business/school relationship, a stage in which we are involved in a political struggle.

If there is a fourth stage of the business/education relationship, it might be that business could revert to the earlier role of simply being a helper, a supporter, and a participant in individual schools—of being involved in day-to-day classroom happenings. That would be a stage of "no news"—of normalcy. But we are not there yet; maybe we will never get there. For now, our chief concern is to take advantage of whatever leverage business has acquired in 14 years of involvement with the schools to affect some fundamental changes.

The Cincinnati Youth Collaborative

Gordon C. Hullar
Reliability Manager, Product Supply
Packaged Soap and Detergent Division
The Procter and Gamble Company

For the past two years, The Cincinnati Youth Collaborative has been raising money primarily for pilot projects aimed at reducing the dropout rate, increasing college enrollment, and getting students jobs. These projects are important, but our most valuable contribution is the work we are doing to bring our community together in support of our youth.

This effort is led by three people: John Pepper, president of Procter & Gamble; Dr. Lee Etta Powell, superintendent of Cincinnati public schools; and J. Kenneth Blackwell, vice-mayor of the city of Cincinnati. They chair a 40-person steering committee that includes leaders from government, business, the schools, and the community. Eight subcommittees involving over 200 people deal with areas ranging from pre-school programs to community support to improving the school-to-work transition.

Our effort can be categorized as comprehensive. We concluded early on that the problems of student under-achievement and school dropouts are multifaceted, unlikely to yield to simplistic solutions, and certainly not subject to a "quick fix." Thus, we are attacking the problems from a number of directions and enlisting broad community support.

While we recognize that ours is still a young effort, we have been at it long enough to develop some convictions about what is important to the success of a business/education partnership. We are convinced that these efforts require the following:

• Strong co-leadership from business, the school system, and the broader community. Unity at the top is all important because differences tend to be passed down and magnified as they move throughout the community infrastructure.

• Broad community support. Key individuals representing a broad cross-section of community support systems must be involved. We have 250 people throughout our community deeply involved in leadership roles on our steering committee or subcommittees. We are identifying every organization that provides youth services and enrolling them in working together on this issue. To date, we have enlisted over 200 organizations with over 1,000 sources of funding.

- A talented full-time executive director. Volunteer effort is not enough. We are fortunate to have Sister Jean Patrice Harrington, former president of the College of Mount St. Joseph, and a long-time Cincinnati educational leader, as our executive director.
- A commitment to success. All the people involved must trust one another and develop a sense of ownership in the process. This takes an enormous amount of time together, so our co-leaders meet at least one half day a month, and the entire steering committee meets regularly and attends a daylong, offsite meeting every six months. I have attended over 100 meetings in the past two years and my boss, John Pepper, has had at least three times that many. Our commitment is typical.
- A common vision, a set of goals, and a system for measuring progress toward meeting these goals. When collaboration and cooperation become difficult, we look to our vision to get us back on track. We believe that our children have the capability and desire to be successful—they will do well, if we give them a chance. This vision helps keep us on track and prevents our differences from getting in the way of what is possible for our children.
- Projects that can provide some "early wins" and a sense of momentum. Particularly important are projects that get volunteers in touch with kids.

We are absolutely convinced that collaboration is the right model and that we will succeed. Our optimism is based on the capability of the children themselves and the level of commitment we are seeing in Cincinnati. This commitment recognizes we are dealing with a survival issue—survival for the productive lives of these young people and survival for the businesses that operate in Cincinnati. And on survival issues, failure is simply not an option.

The Baltimore Commonwealth

Jon M. Files
Vice President—Management and Staff Services
Baltimore Gas and Electric Company

Our schools are in trouble—particularly in large cities—and because of this, our communities and economies are also in trouble. In Baltimore:
- More than half the citizens over age 25 lack a high school degree.
- Nearly half of the city's ninth graders drop out of school before graduation.
- More school children fail statewide reading, writing, and arithmetic tests than in any other Maryland school system.
- Teachers earn $3,000 to $10,000 less than teachers in neighboring counties.
- $30,000 to $60,000 less is spent per classroom than in other Maryland systems.

Baltimore's business community, through such groups as the Greater Baltimore Committee, has committed resources to improve city schools because we believe a well-educated citizenry is crucial to a functioning democratic society. But our involvement has a more self-serving motive: Businesses need educated workers and consumers. The region's economy cannot continue to prosper if companies lack employees with the most basic educational qualifications. A poorly prepared workforce acts as a drag on the economy of the entire region and state.

In a 1986 survey, Baltimore CEOs were asked what skills they sought from entry-level employees just out of high school. As you might expect, these corporate executives wanted workers at all levels who could read, write, compute, and communicate. They said they did not care whether the young workers had been trained in specific skills. Rather, they wanted workers who were trainable. The CEOs also said that they needed young workers who would show up at the job every day, on time, with a proper attitude.

Clearly, business had to get more involved in the schools, but we could not afford to expend valuable resources on a potpourri of well-meaning, but essentially unfocused, ad hoc projects and programs. If business involvement was to make a difference, it had to be both hands-on and strategic. By hands-on, I mean partnership arrangements where businesses go beyond donating some used computers or providing money to buy school band uniforms. Hands-on partnerships involve people working with people.

Baltimore Gas & Electric has partnerships with three schools at the elementary, middle, and high school levels. At any given time, 40 of our employees are working in our partner schools. BG&E employees work directly with students, teachers, and principals. Two of our employees teach an applied economics course in our partner high school. Summer internships are provided to 30 students who have good attendance records. We launched a peer counseling program to encourage students to help each other. BG&E also runs workshops for teachers and parents; pays to send our partner principals to conferences; and last fall collected more than 5,000 books, donated by our employees, to stock empty library shelves in our partner high school. Our partnership is one of 85 that Baltimore businesses have with city schools.

An innovative program called "Our Future Workforce" is being piloted this year in three city high schools. This program addresses the need to better prepare young people for the workplace. A group of corporate executives working with curriculum specialists in the city schools developed a three-year job-readiness curriculum focusing on skills needed to get and keep a job, along with important information on career choices.

Last year, a new partnership called The Baltimore Commonwealth was unveiled. This cooperative venture of city government, business, the schools, and community groups offers our city's students the incentive of a job or college upon graduation. The program guarantees all students who receive a high school diploma and achieve 95 percent attendance in their last two years of school three job interviews and priority placement from more than 150 Baltimore businesses. Those graduates who fail to get a job offer will be provided with remedial academic or job training, followed by additional job referrals. We are making a commitment to see that our students are armed with the tools they need to make it in the workplace.

In addition, Baltimore's business community has pledged $25 million for the College-Bound Foundation—a permanent endowment designed to encourage and enable more of Baltimore's students to go on to college. It is believed to be the nation's largest community endowment to help city students attend college.

The College-Bound Foundation is aimed at the many talented students who believe they cannot afford to go to college and are not being encouraged by their parents, their teachers, or their counselors. Advisors work directly with students, making sure they take their SATs and fill out applications. Last-dollar financing will be provided to those students who fall short of the amounts they need to go to college. BG&E provided some of the initial leadership pledge of more than $1 million to the endowment drive. Our CEO chairs the board of the College-Bound Foundation—a board that includes Baltimore's top corporate executives, as well as the mayor, the president of the school board, and the school superintendent. One-third of the $25 million goal has already been pledged, and we hope to meet the goal within five years.

Another key element of the Baltimore Commonwealth is a series of in-school, after-school, and summer activities beginning at the sixth grade level through graduation. These activities will give our youths the academic and vocational skills they need to go to college, get jobs, and lead productive lives.

Such cooperative ventures demonstrate that the task of educating Baltimore's children is not the sole responsibility of the city's school system. Rather, they encourage key stakeholders in the community to provide the resources needed to ensure that a "guarantee of opportunity for successful futures" is available to all Baltimore's youth.

Many more resources could be provided by business, as well as other groups. We will be turning to our community's museums, the national aquarium, the symphony, the opera, the Orioles, etc. We will also turn to the region's colleges and universities, as well as local private schools, to provide remedial help, tutoring and hands-on experience with computers. Baltimore's excellent library system will also play a role. Other existing school programs, such as Junior Achievement and Inroads, will become integral parts of the curriculum.

Our new school superintendent just asked for a record-setting $60 million increase in the school budget, and he received a good initial response. Even if these additional funds are allocated, however, the schools cannot succeed without the resources, time, and collective leadership of the corporate community.

The Greater Milwaukee Education Committee

William L. Randall
Executive Vice President
First Bank Milwaukee
Chairman
Greater Milwaukee Education Committee

The Greater Milwaukee Committee (GMC), like many civic progress organizations, has spent the better part of the last 40 years on brick and mortar projects. We have undertaken, structurally, many of the projects others have. Only recently, however, did we decide to get involved in the "software issues" of urban America. Number one on that priority list is education.

The Greater Milwaukee area suffered some loss of local ownership during the rust belt reversals of recent years. Although large industrial employment declined, numerous small and growing businesses emerged. Milwaukee's school system has 97,000 students; 150 schools; and 470 central office personnel. Some 60 percent of students represent minorities, and that portion is growing. We have a school board of nine; 5,000 children are bused between the suburbs and the central city. Since the public school system is the principal feeder of employees for local business, stimulating improvement in the design and delivery of a quality education became a logical mission.

Goals

To pursue this mission, the Greater Milwaukee Education Committee was created. It decided to first study the problems facing elementary and secondary education in our area. For two years, the Education Committee worked with school administrators, teachers, and parents to lend a hand in creating more quality in our schools; to be a major catalyst for community-wide collaboration on school improvement; to get businesses aroused, concerned, and involved; and to put pressure on schools and on governmental units for change and reform. It also focused on extra-school support mechanisms designed to deflect the societal influences adversely affecting the learning process.

The Obstacles

One of the stumbling blocks the Committee encountered was a business leadership characterized by inertia, indifference, and skepticism regarding its role and influence in public school improvements, and local government leaders unwilling to involve themselves in a public activity over which they had no budgetary control. The school board appeared preoccupied with a second round of desegregation litigation and the superintendent of schools no longer had the drive to initiate management changes in an excessively bureaucratic central office.

So the Committee mustered forces for change. This change was a combination of relentless private activity, political events, and just plain luck. In 1988, the incumbent superintendent retired to the relative tranquillity of a Midwestern suburban district; a desegregation suit was settled voluntarily; the mayor retired after 28 years in office and was succeeded by a 39-year-old state senator who had a great interest in the schools; the county executive of 12 years was ousted by a 38-year-old parks director, who had a passion for youth employment and job training; a 40-year-old Black superintendent, who had been much involved in the Boston Compact, was selected as the new superintendent. These events helped our education committee reorient corporate community priorities and move public schools directly to the top of our civic agenda.

The Education Committee's Progress

During almost three years of heavy, persistent involvement in public education issues, our Committee developed and promoted numerous promising support mechanisms for the enhancement of the learning process: We established an awards program that provides mini-grants of up to $1,000 to teachers on a competitive basis for innovative classroom projects. (Our review committee has awarded $47,000 to 98 teachers in 66 schools affecting thousands of students in Milwaukee and now in our suburban districts.) We began to be a driving force for change in how business participates in school/business partnerships. We promoted the need for more and better focused school/business partnerships dealing more with those who are not achieving than with those who are making it. We felt that businesses had to be strong partners, actively involved in the goals and outcomes of their partner schools. Now we are attempting to measure whether our resources are affecting student performance, attendance, or behavior. That will determine the future direction of our participation.

Early in the committee's existence, we spent a day at a conference center to educate ourselves about education. We invited local and national experts, and after a long day, several of our members concluded that the problems in public education were so great that the only solution was to blow up the system and start over. At our wrap-up session, those same individuals also quickly realized that we would not know how to put the system back together. So we focused our sights on the existing system and decided to be catalysts for change, sharing with the school system whatever expertise and experience we had with our own companies.

Long-range planning and site-based management became our focal points. We learned that minimal strategic planning was being done within Milwaukee public schools. Several of our members became involved in encouraging the establishment of concise, easily understandable goals and objectives. We also launched a program to demonstrate to the school board and administrators how school-based management could work effectively. We brought in experts from around the country to share their experiences. Several board members were receptive to this initiative and promoted a pilot program for implementation last year.

Today, we are strong partners with 18 school principals and staff who are taking control of their schools with greater autonomy of action and accountability for results. In the midst of all this activity, we found our community in search of a new superintendent. We strongly encouraged the school board to think big and seek the best-qualified candidate. We offered our support to both the board and the search firm to help them attract the best for Milwaukee, and we think the community got a truly outstanding leader in Robert Peterkin.

In 1987, we launched a year-long debate about what kind of program was appropriate to support the at-risk youth of Milwaukee. At what age should intervention begin and how would it be funded?

In 1988, our One-on-One mentoring program was launched. This program provides a support network for adolescent students at risk of academic failure: 400 students in ten middle schools, 40 at-risk students in each school. We are trying to improve their chances of success and expose them to career and educational opportunities. The program is sponsored by the state, the city, the county, the business community, and local professional organizations. One-on-One creates a triangular partnership: a neighborhood, a youth service agency, and a business that supplies mentors —all working together to improve the lives and futures of at-risk adolescents.

Finally, we reached out to the newly elected leadership. We saw this as a unique opportunity of having public chief executives who had new visions and the will to work together and who understood the link between economic development and education. We requested pledges from the mayor, the county executive, and the superintendent to participate in a youth summit. This culminated in a day-long conference on the issues of education, employment, social services, and health. A second summit is planned to address issues such as teen pregnancy, housing, early childhood education, day care, recreation, and drugs. The summits will not produce any magic solutions, but we believe they will get people working together to maximize our resources.

Now we have turned our programs over to the new Greater Milwaukee Education Trust; we have taken the teacher awards program, the school/business management program, the management partners activity and the one-on-one project, and have put them into the kind of community organization that is almost a mirror image of what Cincinnati has: 35 broad-based board members with the opportunity to catalyze the community.

The Challenges

We must begin to think of how we can work collectively. Our summit meetings on the future of our youth must involve the political courage for major reformation of policy both inside and outside the public school system. They must deal with the mechanisms of individual self-esteem, motivation, and confidence as well as the tools of competence—all of which are the foundations of success. All of our children can be successful. It is our societal obligation to provide positive avenues for their energy, enthusiasm, and intelligence. Our future as a community will depend on our children's success.

How can businesses play a more meaningful role? Some suggestions:

• As employers, set aside a specific number of jobs for schools to use as incentives for students; also consider compensatory time for employees to visit their children's schools, and for employees to mentor or tutor needy students;

• Develop a strong school partnership that deals with the needs of the disadvantaged and sets measurable objectives for both you, the school, and the student;

• Become a management partner with a school principal who will have more control of and accountability for student performance;

• Support an inner city athletics or arts project, supplying a coach and providing the corporate encouragement to make those efforts successful;

- Send a top-down message through your organization that supporting schools and education is vitally important to the future of your company;
- Take field trips to successful coalitions in other communities; and
- Above all, be persistent.

We have declared no victories, but we have established a beachhead and have some equipment and supplies that are necessary to make some significant advances.

Part V

Linking Education Relations with Human Resources Needs

Education Programming in Community Affairs Departments

Gayle Jasso
Vice President and Manager
Community Affairs Division
Security Pacific National Bank

"Partnerships" is the current buzzword in business/education relations. But what we are really talking about are operating programs within corporations that in some way interact with or serve school systems. Where a company decides to place such programs—human resources, public relations, employee relations, community relations, etc.—depends on the motives of the corporation, the needs of the school system, the needs of the community, and the resources the company is willing to invest. Regardless of where the programs are placed, however, there is always a natural tie-in with the company's human resources function.

Security Pacific is the fifth-largest bank holding company in the country. We have about 600 banking offices in California, a number of financial companies throughout the world, and an automation company. I manage Security Pacific's community affairs programs that involve our employees and retirees in the community in a variety of ways. Our education programs started during the career education movement, when schools were reaching out to local businesses and asking them for opportunities for students to go to their offices.

In the 1960s, Security Pacific was asked to participate in the Regional Occupational Program (ROP), a California state-funded educational program. This is a vocational program, the purpose of which is entry-level job skills training. Some of the instruction takes place in the classroom, but the majority of it involves on-the-job training at state-wide business facilities. Fifty-five percent of our 600 offices participate in ROP and other career education vocational programs, training about 1,200 students in 200 school districts throughout California.

In 1975, the Los Angeles school district introduced something different—Project STEP (Skills Training Educational Program), a program in which students come to a business for training. For example, a group of 30 students currently visit a Security Pacific automation company on Saturdays to use the data entry terminals. In this way they get access to equipment that no high school or vocational education center could afford. We provide the free use of the facility, the equipment, the training materials, and the teacher.

This teacher is a bank employee who meets California requirements for a "designated subject credential." In data entry, for example, candidates with five full-time years of experience and a high school diploma can qualify for a California designated subject credential in data entry. The teacher is overseen and paid by the ROP. The major cost to the ROP—the educational component of this partnership—is the teacher's salary, which varies by school district. The school district advertises the classes and recruits, and sometimes screens, the students.

Project STEP has 130 to 140 classes every year taught by a faculty of 100 Security Pacific employees who teach throughout California, training over 3,000 students every school year. At about fifty of our offices, Security Pacific trains students for entry-level jobs including bank tellers, computer operators, and credit occupations. The students leave in 15 weeks with a salable job skill. They are trained by experts on state-of-the-art equipment.

We do cooperative education, which includes some paid jobs. We have an Adopt-a-School program with about 15 schools. This year we wanted to show students—whether they were dropouts, high school graduates, adults—how to get a four-year college degree. We produced a booklet called "How to Get from Wherever You are to a Four-Year College Degree," which we distributed to all our STEP students.

One of the benefits to human resources is to have first choice at recruiting those you have trained. We hire about 20 percent of our students at the time of graduation; many of them come back later to work for us. Many go on to college, and some work part-time for us while in college. Altogether, we have 4,000 students that are being trained every year and another 10,000 volunteers who participate in over a dozen community affairs programs. We just completed a study of 13,000 former students and we found 500 still employed at Security Pacific. Added benefits are excellent public and community relations and the satisfaction our employees get from teaching. But the real bottom line is that all concerned profit.

Equifax's Learn and Work Program

Charles F. Weiksner, Jr.
Vice President, Corporate Human Resources
Equifax Inc.

Business knows that productivity comes from people, not machines. In this high-tech era, education is the key to a better workforce. In the near future, one-third of the U.S. workforce will come from the ranks of disadvantaged, inner city minorities. A recent *USA Today* headline read, "Executives Focus on Resurrecting Education." President Bush promises to be an education president. As big business, we are the beneficiaries of an educated workforce. So what are we doing about it? At Equifax, as vice president of corporate human resources, I am the people person. We have started a small program at Equifax called Learn and Work and we intend to make it grow.

The formula for Learn and Work is: Education + Work Experience = Independence. We call this a formula for a better future. Each year Equifax selects, sponsors, and employs minority youths in cooperation with the Private Industry Council and the Atlanta public school's adult education department. These young people have dropped out of school. The program's goals: for students to obtain a GED (general education development certificate), to have a meaningful work experience, and to develop a work ethic. For example, the work ethic means five days a week of getting up, coming to work for five hours, catching the bus to class, and spending two hours in school in the afternoon. One of the keys to the program: It means getting paid for eight hours a day. It sounds simple, but these are youngsters who have never seen the inside of a corporation, and have never seen this as a possibility for themselves.

At Equifax the student employees are interviewed according to our normal employment procedure and are placed in entry-level jobs in the mail room, graphic services unit, building services, or shipping and receiving. Once hired, each student is carefully supervised in the work area. In the education area, each has his or her own program. The four areas in which all students become proficient in are reading, writing, math, and social studies. If they are proficient in one of these, they concentrate on the other subjects. We get monthly progress reports from the school.

At Equifax we also have a Learning Center, where students can take advantage of self-learn tapes, video, and audio programs. We have a number of employees who volunteer to tutor the students. The director of the program meets with this group each week to discuss problems and progress—this is another key to the program's success. Those who complete the program get a GED. If Equifax has a job available, we hire them in full-time, salaried positions. If we cannot at the time, we work with the Private Industry Council to place them elsewhere in the city.

This is a letter written by a kid who did not make it:

> "I want to let you know that it was a pleasure working for you, and I'm very sorry that it did not work out. I realize that you was only trying to help me and I let you down. If I could turn the time back, I would do it all over again in a different way. Me and my family was dealing with some difficult problems, but now we have worked them out. I'm still trying not to make the same mistake again, and I hope sometime in the future we see one another again. I'm still working on getting my GED, and then I want to get my private security certificate. And Miss Lovingood, I think you are a wonderful person, and I wanted to thank you for giving me the opportunity to work for one of the most largest company in Atlanta and hope someday that I get another chance at working for you again. And thank you for helping me find myself. Yours truly."

So why do we do it? National statistics show that 700,000 to 900,000 kids drop out of school (25 percent of those enrolled). Imagine the cost to society of kids who cannot get work; most of them are minorities. The core of our future workforce will come from this at-risk group. In Georgia the situation is worse. In 1975, Georgia enrolled 104,000 children in the first grade. Twelve years later, 60,000 graduated (a dropout rate of 40 percent). No skills, no job, and no money does not mean no family and no responsibilities. In light of these statistics, we wanted to do something to develop independent young citizens. In the past we had been involved in Adopt a School, the Merit Employer Association, Inroads, and many other such programs, but we were not addressing the hard-core problem.

How is it going? Slow, but we have had some wonderful results. The director of the program is a real plus. She started in an entry-level position. Today, she is an assistant vice president of Equifax. Students can really relate to her and to her success. Today, there is real peer pressure to perform, to be on time, and not ruin the program for the next guy.

Camille is one of our success stories. She started the program in February 1988 as one of the original six student participants. She had never been inside a large office building or in this type of work environment before. She was belligerent and had problems at home and with her fellow mailroom workers. Mid-year, Camille became our first GED graduate. We gave her a small salary increase during the summer. By the end of the year, we had hired Camille full time, and she has since received a promotion.

We take in only six students a year. It is a great expense, but if we could get every company to participate, then we would really have started something.

So why do we do it? The following story will help to explain: On the beach, an old man met a young man throwing starfish back into the sea. When asked why, the young man said that the stranded starfish would die if not thrown back. The old man remarked that the beach went on for many miles, there were millions of starfish, and the the boy's efforts would make no difference. The young man looked at the starfish in his hand and said, "It makes a difference to this one."

The Human Resources/ Community Relations Team Approach

Margaret M. McCann
Director of Employment and Recruitment
Brooklyn Union Gas Company

Jocelyn Lewis
Educational Representative
Brooklyn Union Gas Company

Brooklyn Union Gas serves about four million people in an area that includes the New York City boroughs of Brooklyn, Staten Island, and most of Queens. One thing that makes Brooklyn Union different from many companies is our vested interest in the community. We are here to stay and that fact forces us to take action to ensure that there is an educated labor force in the community. Over 80 percent of our employees live within our service territory. Over 90 percent of the applicants for both exempt and nonexempt positions also live within our service territory and have been educated in New York City schools.

Department of Labor statistics show a decline in the availability of qualified labor. In New York, we are particularly concerned about the dropout rate in our city schools and with the illiteracy rate of those who do graduate. The implications of this to human resources is staggering. Applicants today are simply unprepared to do the work we ask. These are not jobs requiring college or years of experience; these are blue-collar, entry-level jobs, like meter reading, which do not require anything more than a high school education, a willingness to do the job, and an ability to learn. Like many other companies, we offer extensive training in how to do the job. We can teach someone to read a meter and use a hand-held computer, but we cannot teach them that they need to be at work on time every day.

Recognizing the need to become more involved in the schooling of our future employees, Brooklyn Union enthusiastically embraced the Join-a-School program. Cosponsored by the Board of Education and the

New York City Partnership, the Join-a-School program links corporations and high schools to prepare students for corporate life after they graduate. At Brooklyn Union, our CEO chairs a Join-a-School policy committee—comprising representatives from community relations, human resources, and, most importantly, line operations managers.

In 1985, Brooklyn Union became involved, through the Join-a-School program, with Erasmus Hall High School. One of our first tasks was to improve Erasmus Hall's image in the community. Like many inner city schools, Erasmus Hall had a negative image—in fact, many in the community felt the school was a liability. We invited community and business representatives to meet with the school principal and teacher and student representatives. Our CEO also participated. The Erasmus Hall Round Table initiated a much-needed dialogue between the school and the community. As a result of the meeting, an Erasmus Hall Community Advisory Council was formed. Projects have already been planned that will involve students in community service. Slowly, the wheels of change have started to turn.

One of the other projects we are involved in is the Career Awareness and Job Readiness program, in which company representatives visit local high schools to discuss how to go about getting a job. We use line managers and members of the human resources training department to advise students on how to prepare for job interviews—how to dress, to talk, to write a resume, to fill out an application. We have also arranged for professional athletes, corporate representatives and community leaders to address students at Erasmus Hall and other high schools on the importance of getting an education, the evils of substance abuse, etc.

Another program that prepares students for corporate life is our "job shadowing" program. In this program, a high school student is assigned to one of our employees. By "shadowing" the employee, the student—perhaps for the first time—sees what an office looks like and experiences what it might be like to work in that environment. In addition, we have an on-campus recruitment program at local high schools for both full- and part-time, summer, and internship positions. We are also involved in a summer employment program for teachers.

In order to establish an ongoing interaction between Brooklyn Union and K-12 teachers in our service area, we recently established a teachers' advisory committee. The committee includes teachers in the sciences, social studies, and vocational education, as well as representatives from special education, bilingual, and English-as-a-Second Language programs. (Some time ago, we recognized that many of our non-English-speaking customers were relying very heavily on their school-age children to conduct household business, such as making complaints and asking for assistance in understanding their gas bills. We therefore embarked on a pilot program to help improve communication between Brooklyn Union and its non-English-speaking customers.)

We have found it important to encourage teachers to take an active role in planning and developing programs. This year, we awarded grants to about 20 Erasmus Hall teachers for innovative projects. These are not projects we necessarily want replicated; rather, we want to encourage teachers to consider more nontraditional methods of educating students. We also recently met with representatives from the Board of Education and New York Technical College to discuss changing the curriculum in city high schools to better prepare students for the jobs we have to offer.

As progress is made and needs change, Brooklyn Union will certainly become more involved. We encourage other companies to participate in readying our young people for the future.

The Corporate Education Department

Badi Foster
President AEtna Institute for Corporate Education
AEtna Casualty and Surety Company

The AEtna Institute was established in 1981. Its mission is to enhance individual and organizational potential for achieving corporate objectives through education and training; to provide leadership on the identification and resolution of business issues involving education and training; to maintain excellence in the design and delivery of corporate education; and to provide a physical environment that enhances learning potential and that symbolizes AEtna's commitment to its people.

Located in Hartford, Connecticut, the institute is a state-of-the-art, $45-million learning environment. AEtna has about 47,000 employees in 8,000 independent agencies—that is our distribution system. Two-thirds of our employees are scattered around the United States. We have made a major investment in the strategic use of education because we have been confronted with a series of changes. The extent to which we manage these transformations is the extent to which we will succeed, indeed, survive.

The first transformation has to do with the revolution in corporate identity—who we are and where we are going. Traditionally, we were a life and property casualty insurance company; now we are an insurance/financial services company. If an individual goes through an identity crisis, you would expect aberrant behavior; the same is true for an organization.

The second transformation deals with the intended and unintended consequences of the rapid introduction of information systems technology. The success of our business is determined to a large extent by how quickly we plan, build, run, and control information systems. We have rediscovered that when you change the means of production, you necessarily change all social relationships. The critical success factors in bringing up a system have less to do with hardware and software than with the social relationships that characterize the way in which jobs are designed and the very meaning of work.

The third transformation deals with the globalization of our business. Traditionally, we thought of ourselves as a Northeast-based insurance company, operating in a sealed domestic market. Today we have an international focus; we sell insurance and financial services anywhere in the world we choose.

The fourth transformation deals with the growing diversity of our workforce. Diversity is often used as a code word for race and gender, but it comprises far more. It has to do with understanding that the values, assumptions, and world views of our workforce and our customers are increasingly diverse. Celebrating that diversity and feeling comfortable with it is fundamental to our mission. The sad fact is that most of us have not been prepared to manage such diversity.

The final transformation deals with the relationship between corporations and society. Limited liability corporations are creatures of society; they have been given certain privileges and rights along with certain responsibilities. If corporations do not understand that they have multiple stakeholders and bottom lines, society will force changes in the way businesses operate.

Given these transformations, AEtna decided to use education and training to increase the willingness and capacity of our employees and our managers to change. Indeed, we became very much concerned about certain characteristics of organizations and individuals who do not have that capacity. We use education and training as a way to change those negative characteristics into positive ones.

An example of a negative characteristic is contempt for the customer. We would like to see solid commitment to and focus on the customer. Another negative is a bureaucratic, slow-to-respond organization, with many layers of management. We want an organization that is quick and flexible, where there is a continuous focus on quality, and where there is an emphasis on smaller, rather than larger, units. We do not want our people to focus exclusively on cost reduction. We want them to focus on eliminating waste, which automatically leads to quality, which quite often leads to cost reduction. The reverse is not always true. At the individual level, we want employees who understand teamwork, are problem solvers, have high self-esteem, and are more than what they do.

Our method for reducing negative characteristics and for replacing them with positive ones begins with the "AEtna Management Process." This is a series of simple questions that we expect our managers to be able to answer.

First, what is your mission?

Second, what are the critical success factors necessary to accomplish your mission?

Third, what factors in the internal and external environment affect your critical success factors, thereby creating gaps?

Fourth, once you have identified these gaps, what are your objectives aimed at closing them?

Fifth, how can you allocate your scarce resources to your most important objectives?

Finally, do you monitor how well you are doing in closing the gaps? This is not a planning process; it is a way of thinking about your business and its energy—it is continuous.

We integrate issues of information systems technology, business strategy, and human resource management into our training. Our education is learner-driven. We have a standardized learning-design model and a systematic way of certifying instructors. We spend much time on the continuous process of increasing the mix of various educational technologies to reduce the barriers of time and distance. These technologies range from our own direct-broadcast satellite system to pencil and paper. The scope of our education involves technology, management education, business education, and a school that we created recently that has received national attention—an effective business skills school (which gets at the question of remediation).

We have been involved in some very explicit attempts to apply what we know. We have a program called Stepping Up. In corporations without a coherent link between corporate staffing, corporate public involvement, and corporate education, you will find chaos. Those three functions must work closely together. We do so in Stepping Up, which is a three-part program. It begins with a Saturday Academy—an enrichment program run in conjunction with the Hartford public schools for inner city seventh graders and the significant adults in their lives. It has been in operation for four years; it works; and it shows that when you put competent public school teachers in an environment that empowers them, and state the goals, incredible progress can be made. The second piece of Stepping Up is High School Students at Work: This is carried out at several of our field offices. In this part of the program, at-risk high school students study and work with us for two years and are guaranteed employment upon graduation. The third piece is the Office Futures program which deals with inner city adults out of high school and works in collaboration with community-based organizations.

We are confronted with a question of political will. The numbers of people involved in this issue and the level of discourse have risen. Senior business officials now understand the scope of reform and what the political costs are going to be. The metaphor used here is "a third wave," but I am not sure that is correct. We need an earthquake that causes a tidal wave before we are going to get the type of educational reform that is necessary.

Marian Wright Edelman of the Children's Defense Fund told me that you can talk about school reform, but if the children are not saved, you will not have anybody to educate. So the issue is to find common ground—common cause. We need to fashion broad-based coalitions that will allow us to mobilize and sustain the efforts on reform. For example, the Jefferson Institute in California has a program called Kids' Place—operating in Seattle, being introduced in San Francisco, and eventually in St. Louis—where kids are surveyed about what is good and bad about cities. The answers are the basis for improving the quality of life. If you make the cities safe for kids, it is good for everybody. This is a working example of how to involve children in policy making.

SYSTEM MATERIALS
BLDG. 250

BRANCH COPY